AN ALPHABET
~ OF ~
SPELLS

About the Author

Elen Hawke lives in England, in the beautiful and historic town of Oxford. She has been pagan for many years, having been initiated through both the Druid path and Wicca (descending in direct line from Gerald Gardner). She is an astrologer and tarot reader, as well as a photographer and illustrator. To find out more about Elen's work, visit www.witchcraft.org/elenhawke.htm

To Write to the Author

If you wish to contact the author or would like more information about this book, please write to the author in care of Llewellyn Worldwide and we will forward your request. Both the author and publisher appreciate hearing from you and learning of your enjoyment of this book and how it has helped you. Llewellyn Worldwide cannot guarantee that every letter written to the author can be answered, but all will be forwarded. Please write to:

Elen Hawke
℅ Llewellyn Worldwide
P.O. Box 64383, Dept. 0-7387-0466-0
St. Paul, MN 55164-0383, U.S.A.

Please enclose an international postal reply coupon, and include your email address with your letter.

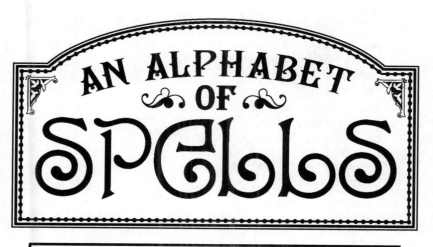

AN ALPHABET OF SPELLS

Elen Hawke

2003
Llewellyn Publications
St. Paul, Minnesota 55164-0383, U.S.A.

First Edition
First Printing, 2003

Book design and editing by Karin Simoneau
Cover design by Gavin Dayton Duffy

Library of Congress Cataloging-in-Publication Data
Hawke, Elen, 1947–
   An alphabet of spells / Elen Hawke.
     p.   cm.
   Includes index.
   ISBN 0-7387-0466-0
   1. Witchcraft. 2. Charms. 3. Magic. I. Title.
   BF1566.H3762003
   133.4'4—dc21   2003051660

Llewellyn Publications
A Division of Llewellyn Worldwide, Ltd.
P.O. Box 64383, Dept. 0-7387-0466-0
St. Paul, MN 55164-0383, U.S.A.
www.llewellyn.com

 Printed on recycled paper in the United States of America

For my dear friend Morgana of Morgana's Chamber, New York.

Thanks are due as ever to my supportive family and friends, and to Karin, my editor, who works her magic to turn my raw material into a finished product to be proud of.

MAGIC

Anybody can do magic. This seems a strange statement in view of the dramatic representation of magic in the media, and the complicated and mystical approach used by the authors of some spell books. But it's true: magic can be very simple; it makes use of natural forces and can incorporate mundane, everyday ingredients. If you want, you may use the tools of the Craft, such as the athame, wand, pentacle, and cauldron, and there are many good books from which you can learn their functions. You can equally work with your bare hands or improvised tools. Choose the method that suits you best, and with which you are most comfortable: you may very well discover what works best for you by experimenting, and your preferred method may incorporate a little bit of everything.

Magic can be as fancy or as uncomplicated as you make it. You can buy specialised components from occult suppliers: shaped candles in different colours, with gradations for specific burning times; incenses mixed at the correct phases of the moon from ingredients harvested on the most propitious day of the week; handmade ritual implements; Books of Shadows crafted from parchment or vellum and written in black ink. Or you can use what you find, whether that be seeds and fruits from the kitchen, herbs from the garden, and any old feathers, buttons, ribbons, beads, or bits of paper that you discover lying around. The main thing with magic is to be creative and flexible, and to infuse the spell with enthusiasm, energy, and a belief in yourself and your purpose. That way you will see satisfactory results.

It's best to cleanse the materials for spells so you rid them of any prior vibrations that might distort your working (see the "Purification" spell on page 83).

Remember that whatever props you use for magical work, they can only do their job if you believe you will get results; coloured candles and fancy incenses are no substitute for the power of the mind. Magic is an energy exchange, you get out what you put in, so if you want a positive result, you need to concentrate hard on your working, raising power, and visualising. The raw energy you expend on your spell will be transformed into the result you are striving for. However, magic is not a substitute for practical actions and common sense, so if you need more money, for example, the first step is to look for ways to earn it, then use magic to enhance your plan.

The power used to fuel some spells is called etheric energy. This is present all the time, in the air we breathe, in the food we eat. We generate more of it through exercise, sex, emotion, listening to music, crowd mood, and so on: you can even experience it quite strongly by rubbing your hands briskly together, holding your palms apart, facing each other, then bringing them together. You will feel a cushiony sort of resistance, and this is the etheric power you have increased with your actions. When a spell asks you to direct energy, it assumes you will have raised power by dancing, drumming, singing, or participating in another activity that increases etheric force. Your mind does the work of infusing the spell with power: if you imagine a stream of white light flowing into a candle held in your hands, then that power really will be entering the substance of the candle, even if your physical eyes are unable to see it. In magical work, the force of imagination is everything. Some spells, of course, don't require you to direct force, but simply to chant certain words, or to imagine an outcome; but even here you will be charging the working with the power of your words or mind, both of which carry their own etheric energy. So don't worry about "doing it right," simply follow the instructions of the spell.

You don't have to study for years to master spellcrafting, though it would be wise to learn a few basic commonsense rules first. The most important rule is that you always specify harmlessness to yourself and anyone else when in pursuit of your desires. You must also respect the free will of other people. A good point to remember is that magic, like any other natural force, will take the path of least resistance, which is why you need to make sure your wording and intentions rule out anything detrimental: for example, the easiest way to attain a promotion is for the person directly above you to get fired; this is *not* an ethical or desirable result. If you are employing magical energies to achieve your goals, then you must accept the karmic consequences of any selfish or careless spells. Not only that, but a badly crafted spell is likely to rebound on you, possibly with very unpleasant results. With a little extra thought and care, spells can be worded in a way that ensures the free will, safety, and well-being of everyone while still bringing about the results you want.

The other important factor to know is that magic should often be timed to fit in with the waxing and waning energies of the moon, so spells for increase take place while the moon is waxing, while spells for decrease are timed to follow the moon's waning energies. The spells in this book will specify if a particular lunar phase is appropriate.

Be prepared for the fact that magic will change you. The moment you choose to take control of your own life by casting spells to alter your circumstances, you will begin to transform yourself as well. Make no mistake, the potent energies involved in magic work on a very deep level. If you do selfish magic, then you will become more selfish and less lovable. If you use your powers wisely, with a regard for ethics, and with positive intentions toward yourself and the rest of creation, then you will gradually and subtly acquire more insight into life, more sense of your own spiritual purpose; you will be a more fulfilled person.

The spells in this book have all been created by me. Some of them were taken from my personal notes and Books of Shadows, compiled over many years, and others were invented recently. All will work if you believe they will. Every spell ever used was written by someone somewhere to fit a current requirement or situation. Feel free to alter the spells here, or to experiment or use them as a basis for your own. The best spells will eventually be the ones you create yourself for a specific purpose or need.

Finally, a few words about the use of crystals and other minerals. Due to our greed for these things, they are now often mined in ways that are incompatible with pagan philosophy. Dynamiting and strip-mining destroy large tracts of countryside and displace native peoples. If you want to incorporate crystals into magical work, either use ones you already have, or buy them from sources where they have been obtained naturally, such as from the seashore or riverbeds, or where mining is done on a small scale that doesn't interfere too much with the local environment. Crystals absorb psychic atmosphere, so cleanse them in a solution of cool water and sea salt before use, and frequently cleanse any that you wear or carry regularly—though be sure to "tell" the crystals to retain any magical intent you have imbued them with.

Abundance

If you feel you are lacking in some area of your life, or would just like to increase abundance generally, this simple spell will help. All you need is a pinch of cress, alfalfa, or other sprouting edible seeds, and a small amount of compost or paper tissue placed in a container or bowl.

Cast a circle if you like, but otherwise sit in a quiet place, such as before an altar or shrine, and light candles and incense. Hold the bowl of materials in which you will be sprouting the seeds. Visualise energies of growth permeating it (you might see these as green or gold or any other colour you desire). Then place the seeds in the palm of your hand, cup the other hand over them, and think about the sort of abundance you are hoping for. Is it good health, energy, or material comfort you want? Be very specific. Imagine yourself enjoying wealth, happiness, or whatever you desire. Be sure that you ask only for those things that will be beneficial to you and others. When you are ready, tip the seeds evenly across the container.

Put your seed spell in a light, warm spot to grow. Water daily, briefly thinking of your magical goal as you do so. When the seeds are ready, cut them and add them to a sandwich or salad, then eat it, taking the abundance into yourself and making it a part of you.

Anger

If you are going through a phase of feeling angry, or someone is directing his or her anger toward you, a lot can be done by magical means to calm things down. (This spell can even work with a belligerent dog or cat.) Remember to look for the cause of the behaviour, and use practical means to back up the spell.

You need as many pale blue candles as you have space and holders for. You don't need any special ritual or words for the magic to work. Simply place the blue candles all around your home and light them often. Take time to be still and tune into the peaceful aura the candles bring into your space. Burning lavender essential oil in an oil burner will help as well, as will wearing blue for a while (even if it's just blue socks or underwear), or using some pale blue furnishings such as bedding or cushions.

This spell really does work. I once calmed a volatile situation with wild neighbours by putting the candles all along the wall between their house and mine.

Appearance

As we all know, true beauty comes from within. If you feel confident and are happy with yourself, then you will radiate attractiveness. The following spell is designed to help you to perceive your own unique beauty, so you can be content with who you are.

The magical ingredient for this working is the early morning dew, so you need to do the spell in the summer. Find a small, round mirror. Wash it in a solution of water and sea salt to get rid of any negativity, then dry it carefully. Wait till the weather is pleasant and dry, then put the mirror in a safe place outside, faceup, at dusk (beware of areas where cats or other animals are likely to knock it down), and leave it overnight. In the morning, bring the mirror indoors and allow it to dry naturally.

The following dusk, light candles and sit comfortably, then gaze at your face in the mirror. Concentrate on the things you like about yourself, your best features. Your mirror is now a magical mirror, charged with the potent energy of the dawn dew. If you are patient and observe your image long enough, you will begin to glimpse the special, loving, uniquely precious person who dwells behind your everyday face.

Now look at the features or qualities that you like less about yourself. Stop seeing them as isolated faults, and begin to see how they accentuate the other ingredients in your appearance. We tend to home in on what we see as personal imperfections, yet to others those very features are the little quirks that contribute to our overall attractiveness.

You may not like that slightly crooked tooth, or the way your left eyebrow turns up at the outer tip, but to others those might be the very things that bring your face alive and make you magnetic or unique. Perfection can be extremely boring.

Finally, try to look at your face holistically, without judgment, instead of focusing on specific parts. Gaze lovingly into your own eyes and see the caring, vital, lovely person who gazes back at you.

Atmosphere Cleansers

If a room in your home seems to accumulate negative vibrations, try leaving a bowl of saltwater there. The water will absorb the negativity and the salt will purify it, rendering it psychically sterile. Another useful purification aid is amethyst, and a small cluster of this will uplift the aura of a living space, though you will need to cleanse the crystals regularly under running water or in a solution of water and sea salt.

Attracting

You need to start this spell about three days after the new moon. If you want to attract something specific to you, such as a relationship, some money, a job, or goods that you need, write the name of your goal on a piece of paper. Sit somewhere peaceful where you can concentrate, then place the paper some distance away from you. Think intensely about your desire, and visualise it gradually moving into your life. Put as much energy into the visualisation as you can. When you feel you have done as much as possible, imagine that a stream of golden light is arching from your third eye to the paper on which your wish is written. You are building a connection between yourself and your magical goal. Repeat this process every day while the moon is waxing, but each day move the paper a little nearer to you. Try to plan it so the paper has reached you by the time the moon is full. On the night of the full moon itself, burn the paper in a cauldron or other fireproof receptacle, thus releasing the magical energy to do its work on the astral plane. In due course, your wish should become reality.

Aura Cleansing

Obtain a large feather, such as a goose feather. Starting at the crown of your head, make sweeping movements all the way down yourself, about three or four inches from your body, working from both back and front, imagining any residue of negativity being cleansed from your aura. If you like, you can burn a purifying herb such as sage or vervain and waft this around you as you work the feather over your energy field.

Banishing

One way to banish something unwanted from your life is to simply wash it away. Imagine that you are holding in your hands the unwanted mood, condition, illness, or whatever. Work hard on feeling it heavy in your palms, all sticky and dark. Then fill a basin with water, and wash your hands with soap. "See" the residue swirling around and down the drain when you pull the plug. Rub your hands briskly together to generate sparkling, cleansing energy. Please don't get obsessive about this: washing your hands once is enough within the context of the spell.

A more complicated but very popular method is to wait till the moon is waning, then will the negativity into a black candle, which can then be lit nightly till the new moon. As the candle and the moon diminish, so will whatever you are trying to eliminate from your life.

Another method is to hold a bowl of soil or compost in your hands and concentrate on an image of yourself pouring your problems into the earth through your fingers. When you have finished, imagine that the bowl is filled with golden light that cleanses away all negativity. The soil can now be used for seed spells, and something positive can grow from this magical compost.

Be sure to follow up any banishing with a positive affirmation to bring in something new to fill the gap. Be very careful with your wording and intentions with banishing spells. You would not, for instance, wish to banish conflict by ridding yourself of your beloved partner. Nor would it be advisable to banish poverty unless you specify that no harm should come to anyone, including yourself, as a result of the spell.

Binding

Rather than binding someone whom you feel means you harm, instead concentrate on protecting yourself (see "Protection"). Binding spells infringe on the rights and free will of others, are karmically loaded, and may have the unwanted effect of tying the other person to you in some way.

Blessing

Magical tools, spell ingredients, candles, and so on need to be blessed as well as cleansed before use. Use an athame or wand to direct power into them, or just do so by holding the objects in your hand and saying: "May you be blessed by the power of Goddess, God, and the elements, that you may do your work."

Bon Voyage

To ensure a happy and safe voyage if you are travelling abroad, ask Mercury, god of travel, or his Greek counterpart Hermes to safeguard you while you are away from home. You can also ask Jupiter to bring you good fortune and opportunities while you are in foreign lands.

Bonds

The old country name for comfrey is "knitbone," since it has healing properties and is used to mend fractured limbs. This herb can be used to heal relationship rifts as well, or to help people form bonds of love or friendship.

On a spring or summer evening when the moon is new, cut a sprig of comfrey about four inches long. You will also need two pieces of cord or ribbon, each about six inches long. Take the spell ingredients into the place where you usually perform magic or ritual. Raise energy by singing, dancing, or drumming. Take the pieces of thread and name them for the two people who want to create a closer bond or to heal their relationship. Twist the threads together, then twine them three times around the stem of the comfrey, finishing with a firm double knot and then a bow. Now project energy into the charm you have made, using an athame or wand, your hands, or even just your mind. Chant three times: "May two be one, may that which was parted be whole, if the Goddess wills." Leave the spell on your shrine or in another place where it will be undisturbed. At the next full moon, tie the charm into the branches of a tree and leave it till the elements break it down and disperse it.

Candles

Candles are one of the most popular ingredients for spell work, the different colours representing various areas of life that might be the focus of magic. Various spells in this book give colours for workings, and there are many books on the market from which colour correspondences can be studied and learned.

Candles can be stored in a special box or other container till you are ready to use them. Cleanse them first by holding them up to the southern quarter of the room, imagining them being bathed in sparkling golden white light, and asking for all negative energies to leave them. Then place a few sprigs of rosemary or sage in with them to ensure they stay fresh, pure, and ready for your spells.

Career

While the moon is waxing, take a new orange candle and a holder, and a length of orange cord long enough to be knotted around your wrist. Hold the candle in your hands and state your intention of finding a new career, or advancing in the one you already have, whichever is appropriate. Be very sure to specify that you don't want to gain your goal at the expense of someone else (getting a promotion over someone more needy or deserving is entirely wrong if obtained by magical means). Be sure to also ask for the spell to work in a way that is right for you. Wind the orange cord around the base of the holder, *not* the candle itself. Light the candle, then leave it to burn all the way down. When the candle is gone, unwind the cord and wear it around your wrist at all times till the next new moon.

Clairvoyance

Use seven violet-coloured candles for this. You will need a bowl of water as well. Do the spell at dusk, as it is a very psychic and magical time when day is giving way to night. Leave any curtains or blinds open, and face the window so you can see the rapidly deepening sky. Light the violet candles and place them in a ring around you. As you light each candle, say: "Bring me clear, clairvoyant vision." Look out at the sky for a while, allowing your mind to wander freely, but observing any thoughts or images that present themselves. Eventually, pick up the bowl of water and gaze into it. See what images or ideas form in your mind or appear to emerge from the water. Finally, put out all but one candle. Leave this one burning for as long as possible. It's important to eat and drink after scrying so that you are fully grounded.

The next night relight another candle and let this one burn. Once more, gaze into a water-filled bowl, paying attention to what you experience. You might find it helpful to write your experiences down after the session. Continue scrying till you feel your attention wander, then eat and drink something to

earth yourself. Do this every night till the seven candles are
gone. Seven is a very magical number, the number of clairvoyance and psychism, and of Neptune, which rules these
things. It also represents the Tree of Life. By working magically with the number seven, you will be attracting its power
into your life.

18

Cleansing

To perform an extra thorough cleansing of sacred space
before casting a circle, sweep from the centre out with
your witches' broom, spiralling clockwise as you do so.

A full cleansing and purification should be done when
you move into a new home, or when you want to remove
any psychic residue from your ritual space. First, scatter sea
salt around the perimeter of every room or space to be
cleansed. Then get a charcoal block smouldering in your
censer (you will need to place the censer in a heatproof container to keep from burning your hands). Now sprinkle on
frankincense, pick up the censer, and walk in a counter-

clockwise spiral to the centre of each room, letting the sweet smoke remove any negativity. From the centre, spiral out clockwise again, letting the incense raise the vibration of the space. When each room is treated in this way, sweep up the sea salt and pour it under running water, then open windows to clear the last of the smoke and bring in fresh air. The whole area will feel sparkling-clean and very uplifting.

Communication

If you find yourself drying up verbally when asked to speak publicly, or if you generally find conversation difficult due to shyness, a speech impediment, or woolly thinking, this spell will help to enhance your communication skills. Communication is a function of the element of air, which is represented by blue, yellow, or violet, according to the tradition you follow. You will need a candle that is one of these three colours (whichever color symbolises air for you). You also need to find some feathers, which can be picked up anywhere. If you are observant, you can find them in city streets or parks. To do the spell properly, you also need to know which direction is east. If you practice ritual regularly at home, then this won't be a problem, as you presumably already know the directions in relation to your working space. Otherwise, use a compass or consult a map of your neighbourhood. The magical working should be done on a Wednesday during daylight hours (early morning would be best). Wednesday is the day of the messenger god Mercury, and early morning is the time ruled by air.

Tie the feathers into a bundle. Take the coloured candle to the eastern quarter of the room, hold it aloft, and say: "Powers of the east, spirit of air, bring me clarity, quick mental responses, and easy communication." Light the candle, put it in a holder, then place it in the eastern quarter with the feathers at its base. Sit in front of it in meditation for a while, focusing on all the qualities of air, such as quick wittedness, easy speech, and fresh ideas. Then snuff the candle. Relight it for half an hour every day for a week, using this time to focus on the qualities of air. At the end of this time, let the candle burn all the way down. Take the bundle of feathers and carry or wear them till you notice an improvement in your powers of communication.

Another way of improving communication is to carry a piece of turquoise or to wear a turquoise pendant against your throat.

Compassion

To develop a deeper sense of compassion, or to bring compassion into your life, build a special shrine or altar on the west side of your magical workspace. On this shrine or alter, place objects and colours that are associated with water and west: things that are green, blue, mauve; shells; water bowls; chalices. Try to find statues or paintings of some of the Buddhist beings of mercy and compassion, such as Avelokitishvara, Tara, and Kwan Yin (or Kwannon, as she is sometimes called); the latter is an ancient goddess who was absorbed and modified when Buddhism reached China. Soon your new shrine will radiate compassion into your space. Sit there from time to time and soak up that beautiful aura. As time goes by, you will absorb compassion into your being and attract more of it into your life from outside.

Computer Protection

If you are using the Windows operating system, you can give your computer magical protection by going into Control Panel, double-clicking on the Network icon, then selecting Identification. You will see fields for both Computer Name and Computer Description. Either or both can be filled in with a magical name (such as a protective rune), and this will help to safeguard your machine, especially if you go online often.

For users running OS X, go into System Preferences, select Network, then fill in a name of your choice beside Computer Name. This is also an opportunity for you to turn on the firewall, if you haven't already done so, and get some practical protection too.

Concentration

Take a small quartz point and cleanse it in water and sea salt. Ignite a charcoal block and sprinkle it with frankincense. Pass the crystal carefully through the incense smoke, seeing it fill with clear, golden-white light as you do so. Your crystal is now charged with clear-headedness and mental focus. Keep it with you whenever you need to concentrate hard on something.

Confidence

This spell is especially useful if you are going to be in a situation where attention is specifically focused on you, such as a job interview or a public appearance, but it will help with general confidence as well. All you need is an orange candle, properly cleansed (see "Purification"), and a holder.

First, mark the candle into seven segments with something sharp, like a needle or the tip of a knife or bolline (the white-handled knife used within circle for cutting herbs, threads, or other things in spell work). Then hold the candle to your third eye and concentrate hard on feelings of confidence, or just focus on the word "confidence." It might help to visualise yourself as relaxed, calm, and smiling while in the situation you fear. Then light the candle, saying words such as: "I light this candle to bring confidence into my life." Now let the candle burn to the end of the first segment, then snuff it out, briefly dwelling on the image of yourself as reassured and relaxed. The candle should be rekindled every day at the same time for a week, repeating the words and brief visualisation, burning another segment before snuffing the flame.

If you need a quick burst of confidence for an unexpected situation (for example, you may be called upon to deliver an impromptu speech), then the candle should be allowed to burn for as long as possible. Be careful, though, as the quick version of the spell can have you chattering away in a very flamboyant manner as the rapid eruption of power it engenders takes effect.

Wearing or carrying carnelian can also help to promote confidence, as can drinking an infusion of calendula, or bringing fresh marigolds into the home.

Creativity

Perform this on a Sunday when the moon is waxing, and during daylight hours. You will need a gold candle, some sunflower seeds, a bowl of earth or compost, frankincense oil, and frankincense incense.

Cast a circle, then sit in its centre, facing south, with your spell ingredients within easy reach. Get the incense going. Hold the gold candle in your hands and stroke on a little frankincense oil from tip to centre and base to centre, thus pulling power in. As you do this, think about your need to expand your creativity, or to spark creative projects. Be sparing with the oil and apply it lightly. Also avoid the wick, as you don't want the candle to sputter. Then pick up the sunflower seeds and cup them in your hands. These are your seeds of creativity, so "tell" them how you want them to grow. When you are done, plant the seeds in the bowl of earth, then push the candle into the centre of the bowl and light it, saying: "Power of the sun, bless my seeds and make them grow, that my creativity might take root and flourish. Blessed Be."

Carefully snuff the candle, open the circle, water the bowl of seeds, then put the spell in a safe place where it will receive plenty of light. Rekindle the candle daily and let it burn for a little while. Each time you light it, the candle will release magical energy into the earth, which contains your seeds of creativity, thus reinforcing your magical aim. Remove the candle before it burns low enough to drip wax into the soil. If the seeds sprout before the candle is completely consumed, then remove the candle and put it in a holder near the bowl. When the seeds have grown to about six inches, transplant them into individual pots, and eventually into the garden or large tubs. As the sunflowers blossom, so will your creativity.

Please note that seed magic is symbolic. If the seeds don't sprout or slugs eat the plants once they have been put outside, don't take this as a sign that the spell has failed; it will have taken root on the astral plane and should manifest its results in your life when the time is right.

Crystals

A lot has been written about crystals over the past few years, some of it useful and some of it wildly improbable. It's true that various crystals and minerals have different energies, and that these can be used in magical work and for psychic development. However, one of the best things you can do with crystals is to use them for purifying and uplifting the energies in homes or temples. Crystal clusters act rather like ionisers, energising and balancing the atmosphere in a room.

They can also be used to cleanse the aura by gently holding them near the chakra points, though you need to cleanse the crystal afterward, and eat something to earth yourself. If you feel a particular chakra is blocked, you can carry or wear a crystal that is the colour of that chakra, using red for the base chakra, orange for the navel, yellow for the solar plexus, green for the heart, blue for the throat, violet for the third eye, and white for the crown. If you begin to feel giddy, spaced out, or vague after a while, then stop using that colour. (Please refer to the introduction of this book for advice on the ethical purchase of crystals.)

Depression

Please don't try to battle severe, continued depression on your own: seek professional advice or counselling. This spell is meant to help alleviate the less severe forms of depression that most of us are subject to from time to time, though it could also be used to reinforce other forms of treatment if you are severely depressed.

Fill a small bowl with water, then add a tablespoon of sea salt, and stir till all the salt has dissolved. Breathe in and out deeply, projecting your outward breath into the bowl. Gradually as you breathe out begin to see your depression as a cloud of murky grey that leaves your nostrils and spirals down into the water-filled bowl. After several breaths, lift your head as you breathe in and imagine that you are drawing a stream of sparkling, clean light into your lungs. Let the light seep through your body, filling you with radiance, life, and hope. Then breathe out into the bowl again, expelling negativity into the salty water.

When you feel "emptied" and more positive, lift the bowl of saltwater and offer it to the Goddess to cleanse, saying: "Lady, accept and cleanse all unhappiness from me." Then pour the water down a sink or the toilet, asking for the water to be purified before it is returned into circulation.

Don't worry if you don't feel immediate benefits from this spell. Give it a little time. If you still feel bad, repeat the spell.

Dignity

If you think you may lack dignity, wear purple for a while, and you are bound to feel a sense of self-respect and to act with more decorum.

Divinity

If you dab a little jasmine oil on your wrists, third eye, and throat before ritual, it will open you to the divine. You may experience this as a sense of well-being, of being uplifted, or of bliss. Pure jasmine oil is very expensive, but one of the cheaper, diluted forms will work nearly as well.

If you have sensitive skin, then simply put a few drops of the oil on a cloth or handkerchief and inhale the scent. (Please do not take essential oils internally.)

Dreams

Charge a small, smooth piece of moonstone magically by cupping it in your hand and visualising light pouring into it, or by directing energy into it via a wand or athame. Alternatively, place it in the path of the full moon's rays to charge it with etheric power. Place the moonstone in a medicine pouch with some dried sage leaves and put it under your pillow at night. This charm will help to promote restful sleep and pleasant dreams.

Empathy

If you want to see things from another's point of view, or just increase your sense of empathy, you may need to increase your perception of the water element and incorporate it into your life.

Light blue, sea-green, or mauve candles, then sit in the western part of the room with a bowl of water in your hands. Stare into the bowl and let yourself relax, allowing feelings and images to arise in your mind. Dabble your fingers in the water, then dab the water on your chakra points; play with the water and get the feel of it. Try to be open and receptive rather than forcing your mind to create experiences. Relax and let yourself flow. If impressions come to you, just observe them without judging.

Over the coming days, try to get out into nature and observe how water behaves when it isn't controlled by humans. Watch the rain, mist, or snow. Sit by a lake or stream, or go to the seashore. Allow yourself to become more and more open to the qualities of water, and see how you respond emotionally.

Becoming more attuned to water should help you to become open to others; you will listen without putting up judgmental barriers. From openness, understanding will grow.

Energy

If you find yourself lacking in vital energy, try surrounding yourself with the colour red, and burn red candles every Tuesday for a month. Both red and Tuesday are ruled by Mars, the planet that imbues us with physical strength and prowess. You could also add pepper or ginger to your food, or drink ginger tea.

If you find yourself getting aggressive or argumentative, it is time to dispense with red and go for more peaceful colours such as green, white, mauve, and blue.

Fatigue

Instead of the usual coffee, tea, or cola when you have been overworking and are drained, try geranium oil as a pick-me-up. A few drops on a handkerchief or floated on a small bowl of hot water will do the trick. As you inhale the scent from the surrounding air, you will feel energised and uplifted.

Fear

If there is something you are afraid of, try inscribing the word on a black candle and burning it away on the dark night at the end of the old moon.

For vague, unspecified fears, burn a grey candle to represent the fears themselves, and a golden-yellow one to help you gain the strength and courage to overcome negativity.

Fertility

Planting corn, wheat, or other grains is a way to promote female fertility if it is done with that intent. All the better if the woman can grind the grains down with a coffee grinder or a pestle and mortar and bake them into bread or other food, for she will be taking the fertility into herself when she eats the food produced.

A man wishing to increase his fertility can gather oak leaves and acorns and put them on a shrine or altar before a statue or image of the Horned God.

Fidelity

If an engaged couple wish to remain faithful to each other after marriage, a sprig of rosemary should be included in the bride's bouquet and the groom's buttonhole.

Financial Gain

If you need to increase your finances because of severe lack or urgent need, then six gold candles burned on a Sunday when the moon is waxing will help to clear away blocks and get that money flowing. Prime the candles with a little olive oil, stroked on carefully and sparingly to avoid loosening the gold coating on the outside, then concentrate on your desire for a release from financial pressure, holding the candles in your hands as you do so. Place the candles in holders and light them, letting them burn for an hour. Snuff them and relight them every day for six days.

Flowers

Learning the language of flowers could add extra zest to some spells. For example, rosemary traditionally stands for remembrance, roses for love, sunflowers for confidence and happiness. You could make up your own language of flowers by exploring the different blooms you find. What do they they seem to suggest to you? For example, daffodils might imply optimism because of their bright yellow colouring and the fact that they appear at the end of winter, when sunnier days are on their way; or they could suggest determination, as they point their heads forward, thrusting through the hard earth, often blooming against the snow. Remember that if you assign a meaning to a symbol in magical work, it will carry that meaning for the purpose of the spell.

Gardening

Your garden, as well as your house plants, will grow better if you work with love and empathy. Talking to plants really does help them grow. Ailing plants can be aided by burying a small piece of quartz near their roots. Burn brown or green candles if you want to tune into the earth elementals and ask for their help with your efforts.

It's nice to leave a wild corner in your garden so nature can work unhindered. Butterflies and other insects will appreciate long grass and a patch of nettles, and birds can nest safely in untrimmed trees and bushes. If you allow the earth elementals this little space in which to work freely, then the rest of your garden will be more harmonious and productive as a result.

Plants can be planted according to the moon's phases, so those that bear their fruit or seeds above the ground should be planted on a waxing moon, and those such as bulbs, which have fleshy undersoil roots, should be planted on the waning moon. Weeding can be done on the waning moon too.

When you put in a new plant, it's good to bless it so you give it positive energies that will help it to grow. The following is a small invocation I wrote when I planted a hawthorn:

Little Fairy Tree,
May your roots be nourished by the good soil,
Your branches caressed by the sky.
Blessed by moon and sun, nurtured by the seasons,
May you grow strong and true,
And grace our garden with your gifts of purity and
Freshness, protection, peace, and joy.

Good Luck

Good luck charms such as a horseshoe or four-leaf clover are traditional. But did you know that they will work even better if you charge them with magical energy and intent? Hold the charm in your hands, state your magical intention (for example: "Bring me increased good fortune," or "Bring me opportunities"), then flood the object with etheric energy by focusing light through an athame, a wand, or your hands. Horseshoes should always be hung open-end up. A four-leaf clover can be placed between the pages of a book, or stored in a jewellery box or medicine pouch, or even kept in the box that holds your tarot cards.

Grief

Currently, there is a tendency to let go of departed loved ones shortly after they have died, almost forcing them to move on and leave their earthly life behind. This is not only hard for those left behind, but very cruel for those souls who are also grieving as they prepare to bid farewell to the home and family they have known for so long. Mourning is a natural part of healing, both for those of us on the earthly plane and those making the transition to the other-world. Pets in particular may need to stay near you for a while as they adjust to their new state of being.

A way to allow the mourning process while acknowledging the life just ended is to create a small shrine to the departed loved one. On this shrine, place photos, flowers, and any poems or prose that you have written to express your emotions. Every day, light a candle in front of this shrine and sit for a while, sending thoughts of love and healing, and asking for those souls already in the spirit world, and who know and love you and your recently deceased dear one, to heal and ease the transition for him or her. Allow yourself to cry, but allow yourself to dwell on happy memories as well.

When we lose someone, the loss of his or her physical presence and energy will leave a gap that needs to close slowly and gently.

This practice can be adapted to help with other forms of mourning, such as when a relationship ends or a child leaves home. You may be angry at the person for leaving you. Allow yourself to have these feelings; although they may seem illogical, they are natural and need to be acknowledged before being released.

Grounding

To be properly balanced, especially after psychic or magical work, you need to be grounded, which will have the effect of distributing energy evenly through your chakras. One simple way to achieve this state is to think of your feet. This should instantly ground you. You can also imagine that your feet are growing roots that anchor you to the earth. Another sure way to close your chakras and earth excess power is to eat and drink something, especially sweet or salty foods, carbohydrates, tea, or coffee.

Happiness

Here are two simple ways to bring happiness into your home and into your life. The first is to evaporate bergamot essential oil in an oil burner; just place a few drops in some water. The second is to harvest borage in the spring, when the leaves are fresh, then add it to salads and teas. Either of these measures will bring an increase in optimism and cheerfulness in abundance.

Harmony

Make an incense with equal parts of frankincense, myrrh, and rose petals, and a pinch of sandalwood. Burned around the home, it will promote harmony.

Headache

You will need a handful of fresh or dried feverfew, a small piece of green tourmaline (a mineral that will disperse negativity without transmitting or storing it) and a four-inch square piece of cotton or linen.

Put the ingredients on the cotton, then sew the sides to make a sachet. Hold this to your head and strongly visualise it acting like blotting paper and drawing the pain away. The feverfew will absorb the pain, and will also work as a natural headache remedy, and the tourmaline will disperse the negative energies so you can use the remedy again and again without taking any pain back into yourself.

Healing

The first rule about healing is that you should never heal others without their permission, with the exception of small children or animals (either your own, or those whose parents or owners have asked for your help), and even then, tread with caution. The second rule is that you should never use magical healing instead of conventional health care for serious complaints; instead, use your healing to aid the standard methods.

An effective healing spell will require a photo of the patient, a black candle and a white candle, and some eucalyptus oil. Begin the spell three days before the new moon, and at night.

Put the photo on your shrine. Pick up the black candle and send a stream of energy spiralling into it counterclockwise from your third eye. Light the candle and say: "As this candle burns, may all illness and fatigue leave *(name)*." Place the candle in a holder in front of the photo. Burn one-third of the candle, then snuff it out. As you extinguish the flame, build up a vivid image of the recipient of the healing being free of illness, injury, or disease, or even of emotional problems if emotional healing is needed. Repeat the candle burning and the visualisation for another two nights, burning a third of the candle each time.

The day after the black candle has burned down, and during daylight hours, take your white candle, anoint it from tip to centre and base to centre with a little eucalyptus oil, then send a stream of light spiralling clockwise into it from your third eye. Light the candle, saying: "As this candle burns, may health, vigour, and joy fill *(name)*." Put the candle in front of the photo and let a third of it burn, then snuff it out, building up a strong mental image of the patient being vibrant, happy, and energetic. Repeat for another two days, until the candle has burned down.

It will take at least a couple of hours to burn a third of the candle, so make sure the spell candle is not left unattended.

Health

Carry hawthorn leaves in your pocket or a medicine pouch to safeguard your health. A hawthorn bush planted near the house will protect your home as well.

Inertia

We all suffer from that Monday morning feeling from time to time. If you feel that "can't get going" vibe, especially in connection with a specific task, the following spell should help.

Set your alarm to wake you at first light. Take a fresh yellow candle, then open a window and hold the candle toward the east, where the sun is rising. Visualise all the energy and enthusiasm of the fresh day pouring into the candle. Take your time, and experience the optimism and hope of this new day. Then store the candle in a safe place.

When you are due to commence the activity you keep putting off, take out the candle, light it, and sit in front of it for a while. You should be able to feel the wonderful power of the dawn flooding through you, but don't worry if you can't: it will still be taking effect. Try to remember the alertness of daybreak, the sense of aliveness. Imagine that you are breathing that energy in.

Now go and begin the dreaded task. Don't stop to think about it, just plunge into the task the way you would plunge into a cold swimming pool.

Insomnia

You will need a lavender or mauve candle, some lavender essential oil, and a few tiny silver stars. You can do this spell at any time in the lunar cycle.

Take a warm, relaxing bath and have a soothing hot drink. Create a quiet, candlelit space. Pick up your mauve spell candle and gently warm the wax near the flame of another candle, then press silver stars carefully all around its length, pushing them in just enough for them to stay in place, but not so firmly that they sink in too deeply and become covered with wax. Now carefully and slowly stroke a little lavender oil along the candle, avoiding the wick and, if possible, the stars. Take your time, and try to maintain a sense of peace and tranquillity as you do this. Put your candle in a safe holder and light it, saying: "Starlight, starbright, bring me peaceful sleep tonight." Let the candle burn for just a few minutes, sitting relaxed and gazing at the flame as you do so, breathing in and out slowly, visualising tension and anxiety leaving you on each outward breath. Then snuff the candle carefully, sprinkle a few drops of the essential oil on your pillow (keep it away from where your face will rest), and put out the light.

Repeat the brief candle lighting, the rhyme, and the sprinkling of essential oil on your pillow nightly until the candle has gone. This spell will work on two levels. On the outer level, the gentle bedtime routine coupled with putting lavender oil on your pillow (this is known to help promote relaxing sleep) will ease you into a less wakeful frame of mind and retrain your brain to accept winding down into sleep. On an inner level, the spell itself will work to bring about your goal of an end to insomnia.

Inspiration

On a sunny day, fill a chalice, glass, or bowl with spring water or mineral water. Go outside and hold the container so that it is suffused with sunlight. Visualise creative solar power pouring into the water, then drink it all, "seeing" the energy of inspiration flowing into your body, irradiating your aura and your whole being.

Jollity

Draw a smiley face on a small piece of paper. Light an orange candle and place it over the paper. Every time you light the candle, you will be attracting an aura of cheerfulness, confidence, and optimism into your life.

Joy

Write the word "joy" in pink crayon or ballpoint pen on deep yellow paper, fold it over, then charge it with magical energy. Carry it with you, or place it on your shrine, and it will radiate its uplifting power into your life.

Justice

Are you being treated unfairly? Are you awaiting the outcome of a legal matter? About to sign some sort of contract? Take the Justice card from a tarot deck and place it on a shrine, altar, or shelf near your bed. Look at it last thing at night and first thing in the morning. Say to yourself: *I will that justice be done; justice will be done.* Continue to do this till the matter is resolved. Please be very careful here: don't confuse justice with winning. If you are in the wrong, this spell will not help you to come out on top; it is concerned with a just outcome, which will mean justice for your opponent if he or she, not you, is the injured party. Be scrupulous here, and if you are in any doubt at all, don't do the spell.

Keeping Calm

If you are flustered, nervous, or angry, the following will help you to remain tranquil and unruffled.

Start by breathing deeply. As you breathe in, concentrate on taking pure, clean energy into you; as you breathe out, allow tension to exit your system. After a few minutes, bring your attention to your throat. Visualise a ball of sky blue light glowing at the base of your throat. Now place your hands there and tell yourself all the reasons you are agitated. Take your time, and voice everything till you feel you have understood the root cause of your anxiety and have expressed everything you can say about it. You will be surprised at how much calmer and less burdened you feel afterward. Now imagine ripples of calming blue, like water, spreading from your throat and flowing all around your body.

Knowledge

Nothing can replace hard work if you are trying to learn a subject or are working toward a degree. But the learning process can be helped along magically if you are struggling or anxious.

Obtain a square piece of blotting paper large enough to write a few words on. Using a ballpoint pen, inscribe the words "learning," "knowledge," and "achievement" on the paper, then fold it over. Pour a little water into a bowl or chalice, then cup it in your hands and strongly visualise yourself as confident, knowledgeable, and relaxed. See yourself gaining the knowledge you need, or receiving a scroll, symbolic of your degree or other qualification. When you are done, dip the edge of the paper in the water, allowing it to soak up some of the fluid. Put this somewhere warm to dry out, then burn it in a fireproof container. Mix the resulting ash with some earth, then plant cress seeds in it. When they have grown, eat them, thus absorbing the potential for acquiring the knowledge you seek.

Laughter

Laughing is good for you; it exercises your heart, floods your system with happiness, and keeps your facial muscles supple and free from strain. However, if you are feeling depressed or down, even funny books and comedy shows may fail to raise a belly laugh. You need to enlist the aid of Jupiter, the god of joviality.

On a Thursday, light purple and royal blue candles, then ask Jupiter to help you conquer your negative emotions and release more laughter into your life.

You might also like to wear or carry lapis lazuli, the stone for Jupiter, to increase optimism and joviality.

Learning

If you are studying, and especially during an exam, keep a small piece of fluorite with you. It will help you to concentrate and will keep your mind clear and calm.

Letting Go

We would all like to believe in permanence, as that makes us feel secure. However, we may lose a treasured possession; a relationship may end; a beloved child may leave home; or we ourselves may move into a different house, leaving behind a set of memories. Even happy life changes, such as marriage or moving in with a lover, can be traumatic. We can't hold on to everything in life, but letting go can be frightening or painful, and the following spell should help you to ease the transition. You can do the spell any time, but it is best to do while the moon is waning.

Find some soft but fairly wide thread. Wool or embroidery thread would be fine, or soft string. Calmly and lovingly plait three strands quite loosely together. As you do so, think about

the person, pet, place, phase, or possession that has left or is
leaving your life. Dwell on all the happy memories. These will
be with you forever, you can never lose them, but life can't
stand still—we have to move on or we will stagnate.

When you are ready, slowly unravel the threads again, and
as you do so, resolve to let the life factors they represent form a
new pattern that is more meaningful for this phase of your life.

Love

It is a violation of another's free will to perform magic that
will make him or her fall in love with you; in fact, nobody
can control another's emotions in this way, and the best that
could happen is that the other party will become temporar-
ily fascinated with you, but when the glamour wears off, you
will be left feeling very lonely.

However, it is perfectly acceptable and beneficial to do a
love spell to attract love into your life. Most love spells work
by helping you to feel more accepting of yourself, after
which you will more naturally attract love to you.

This spell should be done while the moon is waxing, and on a Friday, which is the day of Venus, Freya, and other goddesses of love. You will need a pale pink candle. If you want to put pink flowers on your shrine as well, then all the better. You might want to burn an incense, such as Isis, or one containing rose petals—anything that creates a warm, cosy atmosphere.

With a pointed instrument, inscribe the word "love" in a ring around the middle of the candle. Hold the candle to your heart and concentrate on the idea of love. Feel love and affection pour from your heart into the candle. Begin to build up an image of yourself surrounded by affection, friendship, generosity. Don't visualise anyone in particular. Focus on the concept of love itself. When you are ready, light the candle, saying:

> Love come to me I pray,
> From near at hand or far away,
> Let love grow day by day,
> Love come into my life to stay.

Let the candle burn all the way down.

Magical Catalyst

To speed up the effects of any spell, burn a magenta candle at the time of the working.

Material Gain

Orange is the colour associated with the navel or sacral chakra, centre of worldly possessions and enjoyment. If you find yourself struggling materially, your navel chakra may be out of balance or blocked. An effective remedy is to burn orange candles and to increase the amount of orange colouring in your environment and around your person. Try orange or terra cotta paint on your walls, orange cushions or throws, and warm-toned clothing. All of these will lift your mood and attract material abundance to you. Wear or carry orange stones or crystals too.

Meditation

Burning candles of specific colours will enhance meditation practice. For a relaxing meditation, where the object is to put aside the cares of the day and attain tranquility, then all shades of blue are good, but particularly a mid-blue, such as hyacinth. Violet or white are helpful for visualisation and pathworking. If you want a deep meditation on the profound meanings of life, divinity, spirituality, and so on, then burn purple candles in your meditation space. To focus on the moon, use white or silver candles.

Mental Sharpness

To sharpen your mind and clarify your mental powers, breathe in the scent of fresh rosemary, and add it to food dishes.

Mobile Phone Protection

Type in a protective inscription on your keypad in the Welcome Message or Screen Saver options on your mobile phone to help keep it safe from theft or damage.

Money

This spell is ideal if you want to bring a specific sum of money to you rapidly. For example, do you want to pay off pressing bills or loans, or to purchase something you have your heart set on but can't afford? For this spell you will need a length of gold cord or ribbon (the type of ribbon or thin cord used for tying presents would be ideal) and six gold coins. Feng Shui coins already pierced would work well; otherwise you can place a coin on gold-coloured paper (or white paper, which you can later paint gold), and trace around the coin, then cut out the circles and pierce the centres neatly with a sharp knife or scissors, making the holes large enough to thread your cord or ribbon through.

The spell should be done while the moon is waxing, and preferably during the day. Gather the spell ingredients and take them to a peaceful spot, such as your shrine. Pass the gold cord through your hands, thinking all the while of the money you need. Try to really concentrate on an image of yourself receiving the money through fair means (be careful to make it clear in your own heart that no one is to be harmed or restricted in any way through the successful working of your spell). As you pass the cord from hand to hand, running it through your fingers, you will probably feel the tingling of etheric energy building up. Visualise yourself paying off the bills or loans, or buying the object you desire. Put as much emotion into it as possible.

Now take the first gold coin and thread it onto the cord or ribbon till it rests in the middle of the strand. Tie a firm knot around it, saying: "Money grow." Take the second coin and thread it till it rests on one side of the central coin, knot it, and say: "Money flow." Make sure you space them evenly and leave enough room, and continue alternating the coins on either side of the central one till all six are as evenly spaced as possible along the cord. The remaining words are: "Money spin," "Money win," "Money last," and "Abundance fast."

Tie the ends of the cord together to make a circle, then put the spell somewhere on your shrine and forget about it. When the money you need manifests, you can untie the knots and reuse the cord.

Negative Energies

Betony planted near your home will drive away negative vibrations. These energies were once thought to be evil spirits, hence betony's reputation for aiding in exorcism.

Any of the following incenses, burned around your home or magical space, will drive out negative vibrations: frankincense, myrrh, sandalwood. Alternatively, you could scatter powdered angelica root, or add a few drops of clove or eucalyptus oil to your incense mix. Another time-honoured method is to cast sea salt into the corners of the room you wish to cleanse. You might also want to smudge the area with a cedar wood, sage, and lavender mix. All these methods will act to give the area some measure of protection too.

Noise

If you have noisy neighbours or are disturbed by loud music, shouting, or revving car engines when you are trying to sleep or work, create a picture in your mind of your hand using a volume knob to turn the noise down. This can really work. Often the disturbance itself goes away or is reduced, or you suddenly realise you are no longer aware of it.

Obstacles

Ganesha is a Hindu deity who takes the form of a fat, elephant-headed god. He is the guardian of portals and gateways, but is also a god of abundance and a remover of obstacles. If appealed to, he will happily clear away whatever is blocking your path or stopping you from reaching a goal. However, please approach him with respect and ask for his help, rather than just treating his presence as another spell ingredient. You will need a small statue or picture of Ganesha (these can be bought from Indian craft shops and some New Age stores), three yellow candles, and some red roses (if they are out of season, dried rose petals or a picture of roses will do). Perform this spell while the moon is waning.

Place the Ganesha image on an altar or shrine. Put one candle on either side of him and one in front of him, then light the candles. You might want to burn some sandalwood incense as well. Now write a description of your obstacle on a piece of paper, hold it in your hands, and say: "Lord Ganesha, I pray that you will remove this obstacle to my progress. May I move swiftly and happily toward my goal; to the free will of all and the harm of none." Put the folded paper on the shrine in front of Ganesha. Snuff the candles, but relight them daily for a while till they are gone.

At the next full moon, burn the paper in a fireproof container. Then thank Ganesha for his loving help. It is important that you do this whether or not you feel that the blocks are being resolved. In due course you should find that the obstacle that was bothering you has gone.

Optimism

There are several semiprecious stones and crystals that help to increase your sense of optimism, and it's up to you to choose the one that you think will suit you best, or to which you are most drawn. Rose quartz will give you a feeling of loving security and contentment; Herkimer diamond, a small, bright form of quartz crystal, has a very sparky, lively energy; citrine, especially the warm, golden variety, will bring a radiant optimism into your life; green aventurine is uplifting and healing; orange calcite will have you fizzing with giddy joy. There are many more, and a little research will help you if the minerals listed here don't appeal to you.

When you have decided which stone you want to use, you will need a medicine pouch and some herbs. If you are using one of the golden or orange stones, then put it into the pouch along with a good pinch of saffron, marigold flower heads, and oregano. If you want to work with a green stone, then add thyme and marjoram. For transparent stones such as Herkimer diamond, you will need geranium and thyme.

Tie the neck of the medicine pouch, then charge it magically by sending power into it via your wand, athame, or hands. Carry the pouch in a pocket, wear it around your neck, or put it under your pillow. Its cheerful energy will carry on working for a long while, bringing an aura of optimism into all areas of your life.

Peace

Burning blue- or lavender-coloured candles is good way to generate a peaceful environment. If you can burn a soothing incense such as lavender or sandalwood, so much the better.

An alternative colour for the candles is white, and this brings not just peace but purity too.

Pets

Our pets are precious to us. They are our friends and companions, giving unreserved love and loyalty, and they deserve the best from us in return.

When a new animal comes into my home, I always write a little blessing for it, asking for protection, good health, happiness, and contentment. If your animal wears a collar with a name tag, you might like to charge the tag magically to give your pet added protection and luck. Pass the tag through each of the elements in turn, in the form of candle flame, incense smoke, water, and salt or soil (for plastic tags rather than metal ones, obviously you will have to pass the name tag around rather than through the flame). Now hold the tag in your hands and slowly and calmly think of your pet being protected from harm, being safe and well, and never becoming lost or badly frightened. For cats you can ask Bast or Sekhmet to watch over them; for dogs, Elen or Artemis.

A clear quartz crystal in the animal's drinking vessel is said to promote health and well-being. Make sure the crystal is too large to be accidentally swallowed.

Power Raising

You usually need to raise power for magical workings, and this is often done by dancing, chanting, singing, or drumming. Certain materials generate or transmit power too. Copper, for example, wound around the tip of a wand in a spiral, will help the magical energy to flow. Frankincense oil rubbed on magical tools or scattered over ritual robes will assist the flow of power as well. Magical charge can also be stored in objects such as stones or crystals, and it can be projected into the materials used in spellcrafting, such as cords, candles, and the like.

Pregnancy

If you or your partner wishes to conceive, this spell will help. It is best begun at the full moon, which is the Mother phase of the Goddess. Photocopy or scan and print the Empress card from your favourite tarot deck. Put it in a small clip frame and prop it on your shrine, or put it on the wall above the spot where you do your magical work. Put flowers, corn, or fruit on the shrine or nearby. Anoint a deep pink candle with an oil that contains geranium or rose essence. Light the candle and place it near the Empress image. Ask the goddess Isis to help bring about a successful and healthy pregnancy. When you are finished, snuff the candle. You need to find a quiet space each day to repeat the process till just before the next full moon. Allow the candle to burn for as long as possible.

If pregnancy doesn't occur after many months of trying, don't rely on magic alone: seek medical advice.

Prosperity

The most popular prosperity spells often involve the use of orange or green candles, patchouli or cinnamon oil, various herbs, and so on. Here is a different type of prosperity spell that will hopefully make you think a little about money as a universal energy, and the way it links us together. Do the spell while the moon is waxing.

Take a bill of the largest denomination you can afford. Sit in front of an altar or shrine, light candles and incense, and have a bowl of water, some salt, and ground cinnamon within reach. Hold the bowl of water and imagine purifying light pouring into it from your hands, then sprinkle a little salt into it and stir. Now hold the bill for a moment and try to imagine the many people who may have handled it since it was printed. Really try to tune into them. Wish them well, and imagine them being happy and content.

You now need to cleanse your note of any negative energies it may have accumulated in its journey from one person to another. Pass it carefully around the candle flame (not too close or you will singe or burn it!) and through the incense smoke, then sprinkle it with a little water and salt. All the while, imagine any badness or corruption being cleansed away. Then carefully dust the note with a very small pinch of cinnamon. As you do this, concentrate hard on prosperity. Think about what it means to you, how you would feel with more money to spend, more material benefits to enjoy. See the prosperity bringing you security and happiness without making you greedy or grasping. And above all, see this abundance entering your life in a gentle way that causes no harm to yourself or anyone else. Lastly, visualise the note bringing the same things to others once it leaves you.

The bill now needs to be put in your wallet or purse and left there till you really need to spend it—the longer it is left there, the better, for it will attract more money to you. When you need to spend it at last, you must let it go willingly, knowing that it will bring prosperity to the next person who takes it, and to others who come into contact with it. Those who give generously and willingly will receive what they need.

Protection

If you need to put some form of protection around a small child, a pet, or someone who has asked for your help, imagine that the person or animal is wearing mirrored armour, which reflects harmful energies away. It's best to "see" these energies dissipating harmlessly; you don't want them to radiate out to anyone else. Please don't take it upon yourself to protect another person unless that person has asked you to, as that would be an invasion of his or her privacy and free will. Tiny children and animals are another matter, as they can't ask for help, but even here let your intuition guide you, and if you are in doubt, then don't interfere.

When you leave your home, car, bike, or another large possession for any length of time, you can reinforce commonsense security with a little magical help. Simply visualise a wall of blue flame surrounding the object. Imagine this barrier as being impregnable to anyone but yourself and others who are allowed access. You may also visualise a stone wall, a chain and padlock, or a moat of deep water around the object. Use whichever imagery works best for you. Remember that magic is not a substitute for a lock and key or closed windows and doors.

Tarot cards or magical tools can be protected by wrapping them in silk. Black is traditional, but any colour will work. Use your intuition to select the colour that seems appropriate for each object or deck of cards.

A quick and easy way to protect yourself is to imagine that you are surrounded by light, or wearing a head-to-toe garment made of some shiny material from which any negativity is reflected away from you. Variations on this theme might be a mirror facing outward like a shield in front of you, or a glowing blue, gold, or silver cloak.

However, if you feel your sleep is being disturbed by negative thoughts or feelings from someone else, you may need to do a more involved spell of protection. For this you will need a white candle and some sea salt. Sea salt is naturally protective and purifying, as is the colour white.

When you are relaxed and ready for sleep, sprinkle the sea salt in a circle around the perimeter of your bedroom. Then, starting in the northern part of the room and walking clockwise, walk around projecting a mental barrier of light around the space. You can use a wand or athame for this if you like. Now go to the east and ask the powers of air to give you protection while you sleep. Carry on clockwise around the room, doing the same for south and fire, west and water, then north and earth. You have now created a stronghold within which you will be protected and safe. Hold the white candle in your hands and ask for continuing protection while you sleep (call on the Goddess and God for this if you want).

Light the candle and let it burn for a few minutes, visualising its light cleansing the space around you, burning away any harmful thoughts and intentions directed at you. Then climb into bed and relax into sleep. Continue to light the candle for a few minutes every night before going to bed, and allow yourself to dwell on the protection you have created previously. By the time the candle has burned all the way down, the threat should have passed.

Please note that it is very rare for individuals to deliberately target someone for psychic attack. Most instances of so-called attack are caused by the other person's uncontrolled thoughts and emotions reaching the recipient. The sender is probably unaware that his or her thought forms are perceived by someone else, and there is no harm or malice intended.

Psychic Development

This spell should be done on the night of the full moon. You will need a silver candle, a small silver-coloured bowl, and an infusion of mugwort or Artemisia. An infusion is made by steeping a handful of the leaves in boiling water, then straining. Mugwort can be bought from herbalists or harvested from banks and roadsides, though if you acquire it from the latter, be very sure that you know what the plant looks like.

Cast a circle then light the silver candle, concentrating on your goal of developing psychic powers. Pour the mugwort infusion into the silver bowl, hold the bowl cupped in your hands, and visualise a stream of silvery energy flowing into the liquid, empowering it with the intention of developing extrasensory awareness. Dab a little of the mugwort infusion on your third eye and your throat. This herb is sacred to Artemis, so call on her help to expand your awareness in a way that is safe and natural for you. Seating yourself in front of the candle, gaze into the bowl. Allow images, sounds, feelings, or impressions to flood over you. State your intention for your psychic powers to develop and expand. When you are done, eat and drink to ground yourself.

Another way to enjoy the psychic benefits of Artemisia or mugwort is to burn it as incense, or smudge your aura with it. A word of warning though: Artemisia is used to promote dreaming, and it has been known to cause nightmares, so clear your room of any lingering smoke before bedtime, and wash any residue of the infusion off of your skin.

Purification

All spell materials need to be purified before use, as do magical tools, jewellery, and so on. For this spell you will need a bowl of water, some salt, a candle, and incense. Cleanse the water (either by putting the tip of your wand or athame in it and visualising light flooding into the water, removing all negativity, or by cupping the bowl in your hands and letting projected light flood into it from your palms and fingers), bless the salt, then light the candle and incense. Pass the object through the incense smoke, saying: "I cleanse you with air," then through (or around, in the case of flammable materials) the candle flame, saying: "I cleanse you with fire." Sprinkle with water, saying: "I cleanse you with water," then rub with a little salt, saying: "I cleanse you with earth." If you have other wording that you think is more appropriate, then by all means use it.

You can cleanse yourself in a similar manner by putting sea salt or herbs in the bath. When you get in, visualise the water as glowing with light. See it washing all impurities and tiredness away from your aura. Or you can smudge yourself or ritual tools by passing a censer or smudge stick over and around. Badly polluted objects can be buried in dry soil and left for the last week of a waning moon, thus allowing the earth to draw out any impurities.

Questing for Knowledge

If you are searching for knowledge about a particular sub-ject, reading and researching can be great fun. However, if you want to find the information that is meant for you specif-ically, or if you want the answers to a particular spiritual dilemma, then the following may help.

On a piece of paper, write down what it is you seek. Now fold the paper and put it in a safe place, such as a box or be-tween the pages of a book on your bookshelf. Then forget about it. If your experience is anything like mine, the answer you want will come to you within a few days: you may find yourself picking up a book in a library or bookstore and real-izing that it contains just the answers you need; you may have powerfully symbolic dreams that contain the answer;

someone may come into your life who has knowledge of the subject. If none of these things happen, wait. If you are meant to have the knowledge, then it will come to you when the time is right.

Quiet Time

Do you sometimes long for quiet time but feel it's impossible because of the demands of daily life, other people, and so on? Even in a crowded room, you can attain peace and self-absorption by focusing your attention on a point deep in the pit of your belly, then breathing slowly and rhythmically. After a while, your surroundings will fade out a little, giving you a reprieve from the constant noise of the world. When you are ready to deal with the hustle of life again, bring your awareness to a point just below your navel, and feel yourself becoming sharply focused and aware once more.

Relaxation

Run a deep, warm bath, into which you need to throw some sea salt, some chopped lemon balm, and a small piece of rose quartz. Place pink and red candles all around the bathroom and light them. Before you get in the bath, hold your hands over it and visualise warm, pinkish-gold light flooding from your palms and fingers into the water. When you get in, imagine that you are lapped with blissful feelings, that all tension leaves you and is replaced with contentment and joy. Afterward, you might want to wrap yourself in a warm fluffy towel till you are dry, then curl up somewhere cosy and eat a special treat that makes you feel pampered (chocolate lovers will know what I mean!).

Remembrance

If you are going to be separated from a loved one for a significant length of time, give him or her a photo of the two of you, along with a spray of rosemary. Hold both in your hands and say: "Remember me while you're away, may the heart grow fonder every day." The picture and the herb should be kept together. Each time the photo is viewed, the rosemary will work its magic by bringing your image clearly into your beloved's mind, thus alleviating some of the pain of separation. Of course, a photograph can never take the place of your actual presence, but this magical reminder will make you seem very real nonetheless. Please be sure, as well, that you gain permission from the other person for this spell; there is nothing more unsettling than to be the recipient of unsolicited energies from another person, no matter how close your bond.

Renewal

For renewal or rejuvenation in a situation, burn candles of a spring green or leaf green shade. You might also carry or wear a green stone such as emerald, peridot, or aventurine.

Restriction

If you wish to limit the effects of some factor in your life, charge an indigo-coloured candle with your intent, then burn it. Please don't use this to restrict an actual person (see "Binding").

Runes

The runes, which originated in northern Europe, form an ancient alphabet. There are twenty-four letters, each with a specific magical or life meaning. Study the runes (there are many books available on the subject, and you can buy or make runes easily). If you find that a particular rune fits a purpose you have in mind, draw it on a piece of paper or paint it on a small stone or chunk of wood and carry it in a pocket or medicine pouch. It will attract energies that fulfill its meaning in your life. Some examples are: Othel to protect property; Yr for protection till a particular danger passes; Thorn for general protection; Tir for success or victory; Wynn for joy; Ken or Peorth for luck and opportunity. As with all magic, ensure that you ask the runes to work in a way that will bring no harm to yourself or others. You can combine two or more runes to make an inscription or charm; many people wear rings with a line of runes to represent health, happiness, love, and other commonly sought qualities.

Sacred Woods

The need-fire is the sacred fire burned at the Celtic fire festivals. Pagans will be familiar with the magical act of leaping over the Beltane bonfire to rid themselves of negativity and make a wish for the coming season. Traditionally the fire was also leapt at other festivals, particularly Lammas or Lughnasadh (this was done by country people in Ireland well into the middle of the twentieth century). The need-fire is kindled with a bundle of various sacred woods, including: apple, rowan, oak, hawthorn, blackthorn, yew, elder, holly, and ash. Once blazing, the fire should be leapt in one direction to purify, then the other direction to make a magical wish.

Scrying

Scrying is the act of using a reflective or moving surface, such as fire, smoke, water, a mirror, or a crystal ball, to trigger clairvoyance. Images are read in the surface of the material used. If you have scrying tools such as a witches' mirror or a crystal ball, then they should be washed in an infusion of mugwort/Artemisia every full moon, and kept wrapped in black silk when not in use. Don't ever leave scrying tools uncovered in sunlight.

Sensuality

If you wish to increase the amount of sensuality in your life, or between yourself and a willing partner, try burning hot pink candles. If you want to accentuate the effects, make an altar to Aphrodite by lighting gold and deep pink candles amid pink or red roses on a shelf or shrine.

Spirituality

Search for a beautiful spiral shell or an object that has a spiral formation, such as an ammonite. This shape reflects universal growth, which is echoed in patterns from the armour of the lowly mollusc to the spiritual path of all of life, human beings included. Hold the object in your hands. Study the way the shape curves around on itself, flowing inward or outward, depending on how you choose to view it. Let your perception follow that curvature. Try to imagine that it is huge or that you are tiny and are traversing that route into or out of the heart of the twisting arc. How do you feel? Do you want to rest at the centre or dance out to the perimeter? This shape is the blueprint for your spirit. Meditate regularly using this concept, and you will acquire a deeper understanding of the cosmic purpose of life.

Strength

This spell works best at Midsummer, though it can be done at any time of the year. Gather some oak leaves and bring them home: twigs will do if the trees are bare, though fallen autumn leaves are suitable too and last long after they have dropped from the trees; otherwise you can garner some evergreen or holm oak leaves. Put them in a vase or similar container on your shrine. Obtain a gold candle. Put a scanned image or photocopy of the tarot card Strength in a clip frame by the oak leaves.

Gaze at the card for a long time, examining all the qualities it portrays. Let yourself be drawn into the image so you experience its meaning on a deep, intuitive level. Now close your eyes and continue the exploration in meditation. When you have explored as much as you can, come back to yourself by patting your legs or the floor to earth yourself, then open your eyes. Pick up the gold candle, put it up to your third eye, and see yourself literally pouring the qualities of strength you have experienced into the wax. When you are done, light the candle and let it burn for a while, remaining in front of it.

Leave the image of Strength on your shrine in front of the leaves. Light the gold candle daily till it is gone, meditating on the merits of strength each time you do so. As you incorporate these qualities into your being, you should find yourself more able to deal with ill health, difficulties, and the other ups and downs of life. You should develop stamina and fortitude.

Success

This spell should be done on a Sunday or a Thursday, while the moon is waxing, and preferably during daylight hours. You will need a small piece of citrine, a pinch of cedar incense, a circle of orange material about three inches across in diameter, and a length of red cord or ribbon.

Put the citrine and the cedar incense on the cloth, then close it into a pouch by twisting the red cord three times around the gathered edges, knotting it each time, saying "Success" as you tie it. Then hold the charm in your hand and think very hard about the form you wish success to take in your life, being careful to stipulate that no harm should come to yourself or anyone else as a result of the fulfillment of your magical goal. As you concentrate on your spell, begin to send waves of power into the charm from your hands, seeing this as hot and bright, sparkling with golden-orange light.

When you feel that you have poured enough determination and energy into the charm, put it in the southern or fire area of your room. After a month, open up the cloth and burn the incense in a censer, passing the citrine through the smoke three times. You can now carry the stone with you for added success, or save it to use for future spells.

Tarot Magic

Many people are familiar with tarot cards and their meanings. Apart from their most popular use as a means of divination, they can also be used magically. The spells I have given for pregnancy, strength, and justice demonstrate this. Among other cards that can be used are: The Wheel of Fortune to bring about improved circumstances; The Sun to increase happiness or optimism; The Hermit for inner contemplation; The Ace of Pentacles for successful commercial transactions, as well as shopping for pleasure; The Six of Wands for success. Study the tarot and find other cards that can be used for your magical goals.

Temptation

Is there something you would like to resist or give up altogether? Of course, you need willpower, but willpower alone often has you fighting yourself and feeling like a guilty failure if you give in to your desire. Instead of battling with yourself, write down the name of the thing that is tempting you, or draw a picture of it. With a red pen or marker, draw a red cross over the name or drawing and pin the paper to a pin board or, using a magnet, place it on your fridge. Every time you feel tempted, gaze at the drawing. Alternatively, you could wait for the waning moon and then tear off a little piece of the paper each day, burning it or throwing it away.

Tension

If you are feeling tense, stroking lavender oil onto your temples should help, though be careful to use it sparingly so that none trickles into your eyes. Drinking camomile tea is good too, as is inhaling the scent of crushed feverfew flowers.

The following simple piece of sympathetic magic may help as well: take a piece of thin string and wind it into a tight ball, drawing the tension as taut as you are able to. Knot it to keep it from unwinding. Now hold it in your hands and literally will your feelings of tension into it. When you feel you have done enough, untie the string and slowly unravel it, imagining that your tense mood is unravelling also. You should feel an increasing sense of tranquillity as you do this. Then hold the string under running water, mentally seeing the negativity washing away.

Transition

If you need to move into a new life phase but are finding this difficult, or you feel your life is stagnating, you might like to try some tree magic. You will need a green ribbon, a red ribbon, and some twigs of birch, which is the tree of rebirth.

Go to a place where you know birches are growing, and where you know you will be safe and undisturbed. Take your time to locate a tree with which you feel an affinity; you may think it is prettier than the others, or more graceful, or you may just have the urge to approach it. Sit under the tree and quietly connect with its energy. This may take some time, as trees live at a slower rate than we do. However, birch are sociable trees, and soon you may feel its positive response, or you may find yourself visualising green-gold light. Ask the tree if you can take a few of its thinnest twigs. If you get the intuitive feeling that this isn't the right thing to do, then try another tree, or see if you can pick up some windblown branches. If you take from the tree itself, do so carefully and sparingly, and thank it afterward. If you take only the thin ends of twigs, this won't hurt the tree any more than having your hair trimmed hurts you!

Now tie the red ribbon around the twig bundle. This will represent courage, passion, and purpose. Then tie the green ribbon around, thus committing yourself to new growth. Hold the finished article gently in your hands for a few moments, imbuing it with power and love. Now tie the charm into the tree itself, preferably as high as possible, and in a place where it won't be visible to casual observers.

Thank the birch tree for its help. A positive and useful way to show your gratitude would be to pick up any litter around the area, or to propagate trees from their fruit or seeds and then plant them out in the wild.

Travel

If you want a safe and enjoyable journey, choose a piece of turquoise jewellery, cleanse it in a solution of water with a pinch of sea salt, then hold it in your hands and repeat the following: "Protect me while I'm away from home. Guide my footsteps. Give me safe journeying." Then wear the jewellery day and night till you return home. Throughout Middle Eastern lands, people carry turquoise or hang it from their vehicles as a charm to protect them while they travel.

Unbalanced Emotions

To counteract mood swings, carry a piece of either lapidolite, tourmaline, or rutilated quartz for a few hours a day.

Unity

This spell will help to ensure a successful group or team effort, but you must be sure that all parties involved wish to take part. Take a bundle of long matches or sticks, one for each member of the team. Find a piece of blue ribbon or thread to represent harmony, then tie it around the bundle three times, saying "Unity" on each twist of the thread. Hold the bundle in your hands and visualise all the members of the team pulling together happily and in accord. Now untie the bundle so that you release each person from obligation, then anyone who wishes to leave the group or voice a different opinion has the free will to do so.

Vagueness

If you are going through a phase of being vague, forgetful, or spaced out, you may need to increase the element of earth in your life. To do this, wear earthy colours such as green and brown, take walks in the countryside or garden, and fill your home with growing plants, rocks, and crystals. Getting in contact with earth will stabilise you and bring your energy down through the chakras so that you feel more balanced and secure.

Valour

Find a piece of red ribbon long enough to tie around your right wrist, then cut it so it is about three inches longer. Tie nine knots along the ribbon, as evenly spaced as possible, and with each knot you tie, concentrate on the concept of courage moderated by love and mercy. Nine is the number of Mars, the god of valour. When you have finished, tie the ribbon around your right wrist. Leave it there night and day until you begin to feel less fearful. To further strengthen this spell, burn thyme or dried basil while you are doing the working.

Another way to instill courage is to eat fresh borage shoots, or to add the dried flowers to incense.

Vision

If you are suffering from eyestrain due to too much close work, or staring at a computer screen, here is a magical cure that may help you. It goes without saying that severe eyestrain or other visual disturbances need medical investigation.

Pour some spring or mineral water into a large bowl, stir in a generous pinch of eyebright (obtainable from herbalists), and then place three floating candles in the water and light them. When the candles have burned out, strain the water, bottle it, and use it to make eye pads by soaking cotton wool in the solution. One of these pads left on each eye for twenty minutes will sooth and refresh your eyes, while the magical energies will work inwardly to improve your vision.

Vitality

Everybody gets tired and drained at times. If this happens to you on a regular basis, it might be worth trying to restructure your life to make space for more recreation and relaxation. If you are continually exhausted for no reason, then see a doctor! Meanwhile, this spell will give you a boost of energy to bring the sparkle back into your life.

You will need ten orange or gold candles, a red candle, some cinnamon oil, and a little bit of gold glitter, such as the glitter used on Christmas cards, which can be obtained from most craft stores. The red candle needs to be the type in which the entire wax is dyed red, rather than a white candle dipped in red wax. You must do this spell on a waxing moon, so that the energy raised increases rather than ebbs away again. Daylight hours would be best, though not essential.

Light the ten orange or gold candles and place them in a ring around you. Ten is a solar number, so you are drawing energising solar power into your life. Have the glitter within reach. Now pass the red candle very rapidly through a flame so that the surface melts but doesn't drip (it would be a good idea to place a sheet of newspaper or kitchen paper under your work area). While the wax is wet, dust glitter all over it. Once the candle is completely cool and hard, take a little cinnamon oil and stroke it along the candle from tip to centre and base to centre, avoiding the wick. As you do this, imagine that you are priming the candle with vital force. When you feel ready, light the red candle and place it in a holder in front of you. Sit and tune into the vital energies that are being focused through the candles. Watch the play of light over the glittery red candle. See yourself drawing all this energy and vitality into yourself. Finally, snuff the circle of candles, but let the red one burn down. In the days and weeks ahead, you should experience an increase in energy and joy in living.

Weight Loss

Wait till the moon is waning for this, as you want your excess fat to diminish or wane as well. Please be careful with your wording, as with all banishing spells: you don't want to lose weight because of a severe bout of sickness! The aim is to lose any excess weight, not to starve yourself into emaciation. If your natural body shape is pleasantly plump or rounded, then this is the right shape for you, the one that will suit you best, so trying to force yourself to be thinner will make you ill and tired, as well as gaunt, hollow eyed, and unattractive. The idea is to lose any weight that is unhealthy, returning you to your optimum build and size, not to mimic fashion models, many of whom will suffer from premature ageing because of the unnatural methods they employ in the pursuit of staying too thin.

Inscribe "Healthy Weight Loss" on a black candle. Hold the candle in your hands and visualise yourself as healthy, happy, and slimmer. Then light the candle and let it burn for half an hour. Relight the candle every night, visualising yourself as you will be when you attain your optimum healthy size. If you still have quite a bit of the candle left at the end of the moon's cycle, then make sure it has completely burned down by the new moon (let it burn all the way down in one session if necessary).

When the new moon comes, light a white candle and resolve to make a fresh start with your eating habits, planning a healthy diet and exercise regime. The spell will really work, but you have to help it along by changing your habits so that you eat lots of fresh fruit, vegetables, and protein, and become more active. Exercise suppresses the desire for too many sweet foods and carbohydrates, and it also speeds up your metabolism.

Well-Being

Pink candles burned around the home will create a sense of well-being. Use orange if you want a less cosy but more vital energy.

Wisdom

True wisdom cannot be obtained by magical means. However, this spell can help to put you in the frame of mind to listen to your own inner guidance. It is best to perform it on a Thursday, though any time in the lunar cycle is fine.

Find a purple candle and inscribe on it the sign for Jupiter, which is ♃. Light it and sit for a while in meditation. Ask your inner guiding self to show you the right choices to make in life, and how to pursue your true spiritual path. You should repeat these actions every Thursday till the candle has burned all the way down. Then put the spell out of your mind and go about your daily life, trusting that you will be open to the voice of truth whenever you have significant choices to make.

Wishes

When you see the first glimpse of the new moon, make a wish. At the full moon, reinforce the wish with a spell.

Witches' Ball

In times gone by, folks would hang a witches' ball in the window to reflect negativity away from the house. This was similar to a very large, silver Christmas tree bauble. You can adapt this idea by suspending a round silver bauble or mirror ball in the window. Please be sure to place your witches' ball in a spot where it does not face a neighbour's house—you don't want to send unwanted energies to them instead.

The Chinese practice of Feng Shui uses a similar technique by hanging a little octagonal mirror, called a *bagua mirror,* on the outside of a building to deflect negative chi. If you do this, please don't have the mirror facing any houses opposite you, or you will be sending the bad vibes to your neighbours; this is not a nice thing to do, and will likely bring you karmic adjustment as well (if you act knowingly).

X-ray Vision

If you need to get to the bottom of something, or develop insight into a situation, write its title on a piece of paper. Stare at it intently. Tell yourself that you are seeing into it as though you have x-ray vision like Superman. Keep this up for as long as you can, noting any insights you might have. Then burn the paper and put the subject out of your mind. You are very likely to have a sudden sense of illumination regarding the subject before too long.

Yearning

All of us yearn for things we can't have from time to time; it's part of being human. You may yearn for a relationship, a home, a job, or something that is out of your reach or inappropriate. Magic can help us to attain many of our goals, but sometimes something just isn't meant to be. If no amount of wishing or longing has brought you what you want, you need to detach yourself for a while. Let it come to you when the time is right. Meanwhile, the following will help you to let go so that the universe can sort this matter out for you.

Make a pastry or dough mixture. You aren't going to eat this, so one-half cup of margarine (or butter) and one cup of flour will be fine. Rub the margarine and flour together, thinking of your desire all the while. Add just enough water to bind the dough, then turn it onto a floured board and knead it till it makes a smooth lump. Roll your dough flat until it is about one-half inch thick. Reduce your desire to just one or two words, and inscribe these words on the doughy surface with the point of a knife. Set your oven temperature to medium, then bake it until it is light brown; take it out and let it cool. Break the resulting biscuit into small pieces, and scatter the pieces in your garden or on a windowsill for the birds to take. As you cast these crumbs, release all thoughts of the object of your unfulfilled yearnings . . . just let them go.

This spell makes use of all the elements: the ingredients are earth; water is used to mix and bind; fire provides the heat to bake; you scatter the mixture into the air for the birds (creatures of air) to take.

Yin/Yang Balancing

Yin is the Chinese term for the feminine force, while yang is the masculine. If you feel lethargic or passive, you may need to balance your yang energy, and if you feel restless and can't sit still, then you may need an increase of yin. Yang can be increased by exposing yourself to sunlight, leaving a light on somewhere in the house at night, playing loud rock music, eating spicy foods, wearing red. Yin is increased by dimly lit or dark spaces, moon gazing, eating white or pale sweet foods, playing calm music, burning pastel-coloured candles, wearing blue.

You can also try lighting two candles (the same size), one black and one white, for one hour a day till they burn down completely. If one colour burns more quickly than the other, let it carry on burning after the other is extinguished, snuffing it when the two are the same height once more.

Zeal

Zeal is the fuel that drives spells. If you can't get worked up about your magic, then you are unlikely to have the necessary focus and energy to carry the project through. To realise a goal, you need to get enthusiastic about it. This is not the same as being obsessive, when you wear yourself out longing for the impossible or the inappropriate. If you feel lacking in drive but know you have to work that spell now, try this: go outside in the fresh air and pant rapidly five times (don't do it more than this or you will feel dizzy); come inside and stand with your feet together, head back, and arms raised so that your body forms a letter Y; stand like this till you feel energy travelling down your arms and into your system. You are now charged and can carry out your magical work as usual.

Zest for Life

This very simple spell can help you to rekindle your joy in life if you are feeling flat or out of sorts. You should purchase some mandarin oil (the diluted versions work fine). Simply dab some oil on a clean piece of cloth and inhale the scent, seeing, as you do so, a mental picture of yourself jumping for joy, dancing around, flinging your arms out, or whatever image represents being happy and carefree. Do this whenever you feel inertia or boredom creeping up on you.

AFTERWORD

For newcomers to magical practice, I hope this little book has enabled you to see that spellwork is both safe and enjoyable if approached with common sense and integrity. Working magic will expand your imaginative faculties and help you to clear the blocks in various areas of your life (providing, of course, that you allow this expansion and growth to take place!).

For those of you to whom magic is already an active and rewarding part of life, hopefully you will have found some new ideas to supplement your existing practice or to provide fresh inspiration.

There follows a section on circle casting for people who are beginners, or who would like to refresh their memories or try my method instead of their own. It is based on the

Gardnerian/Alexandrian model, but can be adapted and changed to fit personal taste and needs.

Casting the Circle

You will need: four candles for the quarters (white ones will do, or yellow for east, red for south, blue for west, and green for north); incense and a charcoal briquette in a heatproof container, or else a joss stick; matches; a bowl of water; a bowl of salt; a drum or other instrument to raise energy (your voice or clapping hands will do); and the ingredients the spell calls for.

- Prepare for your spellwork with a relaxing, cleansing bath, which will mark the transition between the everyday world and the realm of magic.

- Place the candles in holders in the eastern, southern, western, and northern parts of the room (use a compass if you aren't sure where these are). These can now be lit.

- Light the charcoal.

- Stand upright with the feet slightly apart.

- Relax and begin to breathe slowly and deeply.

- As you breathe out, let any tension and anxiety leave you.

- Feel your feet begin to "root" into the floor and the earth beneath.

- Start to draw up bright energy so that you are both grounding yourself and replenishing your energies with earth energy.

- Now put a sprinkling of incense on the charcoal.

- Hold the bowl of water in your hands and imagine that it is being filled with cleansing light.

- Do the same with the salt.

- Now add a pinch of salt to the water, then stir.

- Walk around the edge of the room (or the area of the room in which you intend to work), beginning in the east or north, sprinkling salty water as you go.

- Now do the same with the censer, wafting incense around the edge of your intended circle.

- You are now ready to cast your circle, walking around exactly as you did with the incense and water; but this time you should hold out a finger and imagine bright light flowing from it, creating a magical barrier; or you could visualise some other form of perimeter, such as a wall or a drift of smoke.

- The next step is to balance your circle by walking to each quarter in turn and visualising the elements, so that you would think of air or wind or clouds in the east, fire or sun in the south, water in the west, and earth or rocks, stones or crystals in the north.

- The last step before working your spell is to raise some magical energy by drumming (or playing another musical instrument) or by clapping, dancing, singing, or shaking a gourd or rattle.

- Now do your magical work.

- When you have finished, you will need to dismantle the circle. Do this by walking around again, starting with the east and imagining that each quarter, as you come to it, is fading back so that the qualities of air, then fire (when you reach that part of the circle), then water, then earth lose their spotlight focus and become part of the everyday mix of the elements that we normally experience.

- Make sure you eat and drink to properly ground yourself, otherwise you might become spacey after magical work.

That's all there is to it, though you can elaborate as you grow more confident. Read about other people's methods and experiment, trying everything out for yourself over time.

INDEX